Walk Around

A-4 Skyhawk

By Lou Drendel
Color by Lou Drendel and Don Greer
Illustrated by David Gebhardt and Darren Glenn
Editor: J. Michael McMurtrey

D1613816

Walk Around Number 41

squadron/signal publications

Introduction

"Scooter," "Ford," "Tinker Toy," "Bantam Bomber," "Heinemann's Hot Rod." All were nicknames for the Douglas A-4 Skyhawk. But an even more appropriate appellation, bestowed by Skyhawk pilots, is "The Ferrari Of Airplanes."

The A-4 Skyhawk is one of the most successful modern combat aircraft ever built. The Skyhawk production run spanned 25 years, during which 2,960 were built and operated by the U.S. Navy and Marines as well as the Air Forces of Australia, New Zealand, Israel, Malaysia, Argentina, Singapore, Brazil, Indonesia, and Kuwait.

The Skyhawk was conceived during a time of burgeoning carrier jet operations. Unlike many of its contemporaries, it was designed from the outset as a lightweight attack aircraft. (The Skyhawk was developed in tandem with the A-3 Skywarrior, a twin-engine bomber with a maximum take-off weight of 82,500 pounds compared to the A-4B's maximum of 22,500 pounds.) In the early 1950s, most of the Navy's carriers were of World War II vintage, and smaller, lighter, more maneuverable aircraft were an absolute operational necessity.

Ed Heinemann

In January 1952, Ed Heinemann, chief engineer of the Douglas El Segundo Division, met with Rear Admiral Apollo Soucek, representing the Chief of the Naval Bureau of Aeronautics (BuAer). Heinemann proposed a new, lightweight, jet-powered attack airplane. On 12 June 1952, BuAer issued a contract for the prototype, specifying a maximum speed of 500 mph, a 460-mile operating radius, a 2,000-pound bomb capacity, and a maximum cost of $1 million per aircraft. The XA-4D-1 beat the speed requirement by a wide margin, and the first 500 production aircraft were produced at a cost of $860,000 each. Review of the basic design resulted in a further order for 19 A-4s in October 1952.

Naval aircraft designations prior to 1962 included references to the mission and manufacturer. Thus the Skyhawk was designated A4D-1: A (attack) 4 (fourth aircraft from this manufacturer under the new designator) D (Douglas) -1 (first example of the type.) After 1962, the designators were simplified, and the A4D-1 became the A-4A, the A4D-2 became the A-4B, and the A4D-2N became the A-4C. The latter was designed with minimal all-weather equipment, including an autopilot, all-attitude gyro system, low altitude bombing system, terrain clearance radar, and angle of attack indexer. From 1969 to 1972, 100 A-4Cs were upgraded to A-4L configuration for Naval Air Reserve squadrons.

The A4D-5, later designated A-4E, was equipped with the lighter, more powerful Pratt & Whitney J52-P6A engine. It had a redesigned fuselage center section and inlet ducting, two additional wing hard points, and upgrades to the navigation and weapons systems. The A-4F added nose wheel steering, wing lift spoilers, and the Escapac 1-C3 ejection seat. The humpback avionics pod of the A-4F was eventually retrofitted to all A-4Es, and 100 of the A-4Fs were retrofitted with the more powerful J52-P408 engine, becoming "Super Foxes," and 18 of these became the eventual mount of the Blue Angels.

Two-seat Skyhawks were built beginning in 1964. Designed as trainers, they were ultimately used in a wide variety of missions, including forward air controller (FAC), utility, and aggressor missions. TA-4E, F, and J versions were built.

Front Cover: VA-46 pilot Lt. Cmdr. John S. McCain III stands in front of his assigned A-4E Skyhawk, BuNo 149996/AA-416, aboard USS *Forrestal* in July 1967. The son and grandson of career Navy officers, Lt. Cmdr. McCain was shot down over North Vietnam and spent six years as a prisoner of war. He was later elected to the United States Senate from Arizona. The Skyhawk was destroyed in the *Forrestal* fire of July 29, 1967.

If you have any photographs of aircraft, armor, soldiers or ships of any nation, particularly wartime snapshots, why not share them with us and help make Squadron/Signal's books all the more interesting and complete in the future? Any photograph sent to us will be copied and the original returned. The donor will be fully credited for any photos used. Please send them to:

Squadron/Signal Publications, Inc.
1115 Crowley Drive
Carrollton, TX 75011-5010

Если у вас есть фотографии самолётов, вооружения, солдат или кораблей любой страны, особенно, снимки времён войны, поделитесь с нами и помогите сделать новые книги издательства Эскадрон/Сигнал еще интереснее. Мы переснимем ваши фотографии и вернем оригиналы. Имена приславших снимки будут сопровождать все опубликованные фотографии. Пожалуйста, присылайте фотографии по адресу:

Squadron/Signal Publications, Inc.
1115 Crowley Drive
Carrollton, TX 75011-5010

軍用機、装甲車両、兵士、軍艦などの写真を所持しておられる方はいらっしゃいませんか？どの国のものでも結構です。作戦中に撮影されたものが特に良いのです。Squadron/Signal社の出版する刊行物において、このような写真は内容を一層充実し、興味深くすることができます。当方にお送り頂いた写真は、複写の後お返しいたします。出版物中に写真を使用した場合は、必ず提供者のお名前を明記させて頂きます。お写真は下記にご送付ください。

Squadron/Signal Publications, Inc.
1115 Crowley Drive
Carrollton, TX 75011-5010

Acknowledgements:

As always, I am indebted to several individuals for their generosity and willingness to share their photos. Ted Carlson, Norm Taylor, John Gourley, Jim Hawkins, Andre Jans, and Peter Steendam made the task of photo-collecting easy. Ra'anan Weiss went out of his way to obtain permission to photograph Israeli Skyhawks, then did the job for me. Except for his own book on the A-4, these are seldom-seen views of combat-veteran Skyhawks.

Rear Cover: A-4M of the 'Flying Wing' squadron of the Israeli Air Force (Heyl ha'Avir), armed with 4 Mk-84 Laser-Guided Bombs (LGB).

The Douglas XA4D-1 was test flown for the first time on 22 June 1954 by company test pilot Bob Rahn. The nose probe was later removed. The XA4D-1 was powered by a 7,700 lb thrust J65-W16A engine. There was no radar, no navigation computer, no nosewheel steering, no spoilers, no drag chute, no ILS, and no electronic counter-measures, but it was capable of delivering a nuclear weapon, using the Aero 18B LABS computer. (Douglas)

With the nose probe removed, the A4D-1 (A-4A) assumed the classic shape and size of the enduring Skyhawk design. Although the Skyhawk would grow extra bulges and ultimately have five hardpoints, the basic airframe remained unchanged, another testament to the genius of Ed Heinemann and his design team at Douglas Aircraft Company. A total of 166 'A' models were built. (Douglas)

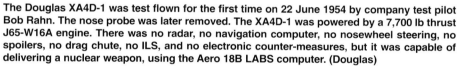

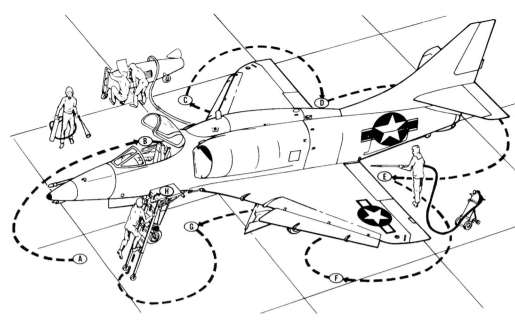

The inspiration for the 'Walk Around' series is illustrated by the above diagram, which shows the route of the exterior inspection performed by Skyhawk pilots during their pre-flight checks. Key: A. Forward fuselage; B. Right-hand wheel well; C. Right wing; D. Aft fuselage and tail section; E. Left wing; F. Left-hand wheel well; G. Center fuselage underside; H. Cockpit area.

The A4D-2 (A-4B) incorporated the AN/ASN-19A navigation computer, AN/APN-141 radar altimeter, powered elevator controls, and eventually aerial refueling capability. Later 'B' models were powered by the more powerful 8,400 lb thrust J-65-W-20. A total of 542 'B' models were manufactured. The 'B' model also introduced the vortex generators on top of the wings, which smoothed airflow and reduced airframe buffet at certain airspeeds. (Douglas)

An A-4C (BuNo 148483) of VA-34 'Blue Blasters' from USS *Forrestal* (CVA-59) in the markings of the air wing commander (CAG). It carries a 'Tonkin Gulf Yacht Club' patch on the fuselage. A total of 638 A-4Cs (designated A4D-2N and A4D-3 prior to 1962) were built. The A-4C was the first version of the Skyhawk to see combat and the first version to include radar (AN-APG-53A) and the capability to fire the AIM-9 Sidewinder air-to-air missile.

A-4C (BuNo 145111) of VA-195 'Dambusters.' From July 1962 to August 1968, VA-195 made five WestPac deployments in their A-4Cs as part of CVW-19, operating from USS *Bon Homme Richard* (CVA-31) and USS *Ticon-deroga* (CVA-14).

▲ The A4B is easily recognizable by its much shorter nose. Differences from the A4A (A4D-1) include a refueling probe and 'vaned' rudder. The A4B (A4D-2) also had the capability to carry external fuel tanks, giving it a total of 1,695 gallons of useable fuel.

◄ VA-76 'Fighting Spirits' flew the A-4B from May of 1959 until March of 1962, when they transitioned to the A-4C (A4D-2N). VA-76 was disestablished in 1969.

▼ VA-113 'Stingers' flew the Skyhawk from 1958 to 1968, beginning with the A4D-1 and ending with the A4-F. They flew the A-4C in 1966-67 with CVW-9 aboard USS Enterprise (CVAN-65). The A-4C was the first Skyhawk with limited night/all-weather capability, utilizing the APG-53 Radar. A-4Cs were equipped with the J-65-W-16A engine, which required redesign of the intakes. First flight of the A-4C was 21 August 1958, with first fleet deliveries going to VMA-225 in February 1960.

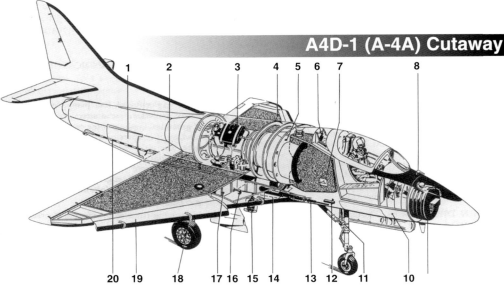

A4D-1 (A-4A) Cutaway

1. Speedbrake
2. Aft engine compartment access door
3. Oil tank
4. Integral wing tank
5. Fuel nozzle grounding receptacle
6. Cockpit canopy air bungee cylinder
7. External canopy jettison handle
8. Pitot tube
9. AN/ASQ-17 integrated electronics center
10. Static vent
11. Approach light
12. Emergency generator
13. Mk 12 Mod 0 20 mm gun
14. Forward engine compartment and accessory section access door
15. External pneumatic starter
16. Catapult hook
17. Fuel nozzle grounding receptacle
18. Barricade strap detent
19. Wing slat
20. Arresting hook

▲ VMA-225 was the first fleet squadron to receive the A4D-2N (A4-C). They operated from MCAS Cherry Point, North Carolina. The A4D-2N (A-4C) also added an autopilot, radar altimeter, angle of attack (AOA) indicator, and several new instruments. Additional improvements over the 'B' model included a new ejection seat and the ability to deliver the AGM-45 Shrike Anti--Radiation Missile. Rocket pods are the 19-shot Aero 7D model with 2.75-inch Folding-Fin Aerial Rockets (FFAR) (USMC)

◄ The 'Bengals' of VMA-224 were the first Marine A-4 Skyhawk squadron. They flew the Skyhawk for ten years, home-based at MCAS El Toro, California, before transitioning to the A-6 Intruder. Smooth rudder, lack of refueling probe, and snug engine intakes mark this as an early A4D-1.

▲ Marines experimented with jet-assisted take-off (JATO) bottles, manufactured by Aerojet General Corporation. This A-4B of VMA-332 rockets off during Operation Blue Star on Taiwan in 1960. (USMC)

▶ A-4C of VMA-223 at NAHA, Okinawa in 1968. (Charles B. Mayer)

▼ The last two Douglas bombers to be developed were the A-3 and A-4. An A-4B of VA-163 flies wing on an A-3B of VAH-4 during the 1964 Westpac deployment. (U.S. Navy via Lt. Cmdr. R. J. Lippincott.)

▸ An A-4C of VMA-131 taxies at Willow Grove, Pennsylvania.

▾ The Blue Angels replaced their F-4J Phantoms with Skyhawks in 1974. Modifications to the Blues' A-4Fs included removal of the avionics hump, removal of the ECM antennas, addition of a brake chute, bolting the leading-edge slats shut, removal of the 20mm guns, extending the port gun fairing to accommodate a fold-in boarding ladder, addition of a smoke generating tank and tube, removal and/or fairing over the flare launchers (aft fuselage under the speed brakes), removal of wing ordnance pylons 1, 2, 4, and 5 (the centerline station was retained), and addition of an inverted fuel system. The Blues flew the Skyhawk until 1986, when they transitioned to the F/A-18 Hornet.

▾ An A-4F of the 'Diamondbacks' at MARTD Willow Grove in the 1970s. VMA-131 flew all models of the Skyhawk, from the 'B' through the 'M.' The last Marine Skyhawks were retired at Willow Grove in June 1994. (Jim Hawkins via John Gourley)

An A-4E of VA-106 'Gladiators.' VA-106 flew the A-4E on two Westpac/Vietnam combat cruises: from 6 June 1967 to 15 September 1967, assigned to CVW-17 aboard USS Forrestal (CVA 59), and from 4 June 1968 to 8 February 1969, assigned to CVW-10 aboard USS Intrepid (CVS 11).

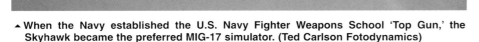

▲ When the Navy established the U.S. Navy Fighter Weapons School 'Top Gun,' the Skyhawk became the preferred MIG-17 simulator. (Ted Carlson Fotodynamics)

▸ Top Gun used several versions of the A-4 in a wide variety of camouflage schemes, some belonging to actual potential adversaries, and some created for their effectiveness. (Ted Carlson Fotodynamics)

To meet training needs and to release single-seat airframes for needed use in the Vietnam War, the Skyhawk contract was modified in 1964 to permit construction of a two-seat version. Two incomplete airframes, BuNos 152102 and 152103, were taken off the A-4E production line and designated as TA-4E prototypes. To allow for a second cockpit, and necessary controls and instrumentation, a 28-inch section was inserted to lengthen the fuselage. The Pratt & Whitney 9,300 lb thrust J52 engine was selected to power the 'T' version. Other modifications included Escapac 1C-3 ejection seats, wing lift spoilers, and nose wheel steering. The first TA-4E flight occurred on June 30, 1965. TA-4E version was redesignated TA-4F and the first of the two-seaters was delivered to VA-125 at NAS Lemoore in May 1966.

▲ Twenty-three TA-4Fs were converted to OA-4Ms for FastFAC (Fast Forward Air Controller) missions in the Vietnam War. The OA-4M was basically a TA-4F equipped with A-4M electronics. Four TA-4Fs, redesignated EA-4F, were equipped with sophisticated electronic equipment for fleet training. Most other TA-4Fs eventually were converted for training purposes and redesignated TA-4J. This TA-4J was flown by the commanding officer of VC-1 at NAS Barbers Point, Hawaii.

▼ The Marines made extensive use of the TA-4 as a Fast FAC in Vietnam. This TA-4F was flown by H&MS-15 at Naval Air Station Atsugi, Japan. (Norm Taylor)

▼ Navy Attack Squadron 126 (VA-126) was established about 1959 with the Grumman TF-9 Cougar for fleet instrument training. By 1963, VA-126 was flying the Skyhawk. When the Skyhawk was being replaced as the fleet attack aircraft in 1967, VA-126 was redesignated VF-126, with the mission to provide adversary training for the Pacific Fleet. The Skyhawk was chosen as the 'bandit' aircraft because of the similarity to a MiG in its small size, maneuverability, and smokeless exhaust. VF-126 started providing the adversary mission from Miramar in April 1967 and continued until it was disestablished in April 1994.

11

The refueling probe nozzle on all models of the Skyhawk from 'B' to 'M' is the same. The refueling boom was 'bent' outward on later models to prevent interference with the APG-53 radar of the A-4M. During air refueling, fuel flows through the receiver aircraft's probe nozzle under pressure and is distributed to each tank in the same manner as it is through the pressure fueling receptacle during ground refueling.

'Glass' nose in the A-4M houses the ARBS TV sensor and Laser Spot Tracker (LST). Antennas on either side are for the ALR-45 radar warning system. (Ted Carlson Fotodynamics)

The antennas under the nose of the A-4M are for the ALQ-126 deception jammer trans- mitter and receiver. (Ted Carlson Fotodynamics)

The Israeli Skyhawk nose section is hinged in two sections to allow access to the radar and laser targeting systems. The IDF AF first received the Skyhawk in 1967. The IDF version had much of the U.S. offensive capability removed and added a brake chute and AN/ARC-51A UHF antenna at the top of the vertical stabilizer, which resulted in the squared-off vertical fin of Israeli A-4Fs. (Ra'anan Weiss)

The starboard fuselage forward of the wing shows open access panels, including the extended emergency ram air turbine generator. (Ra'anan Weiss)

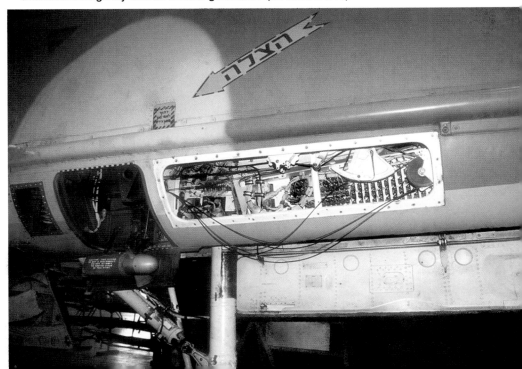

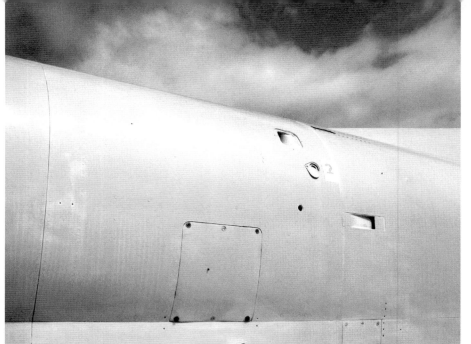

▲ The port nose (above) and mid-fuselage (right) of the A4D-1 (A-4A) show a relatively clean configuration compared to later versions. (Lou Drendel)

▸ Access panels on port and starboard sides of all Skyhawks provide access to engine controls. (Ra'anan Weiss)

▾ A-4M of the Israeli Air Force. Like all Skyhawk variants, engine changes are accomplished by removal of the aft fuselage.

▼ The Israeli A-4M emergency air turbine is on the starboard side inboard of the 30 mm cannon. It can be extended into the slipstream, where the propeller is driven to provide power in the case of generator failure. (All photos this page: Ra'anan Weiss)

The A-4M uses the Pratt & Whitney J52-P-408 engine.

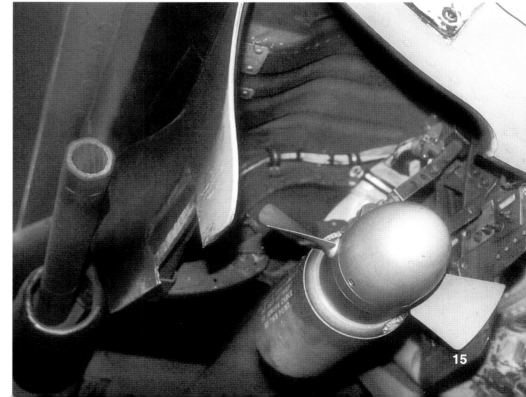

15

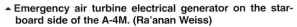

▲ Emergency air turbine electrical generator on the starboard side of the A-4M. (Ra'anan Weiss)

▲ All versions of the Skyhawk use fuselage speed brakes.

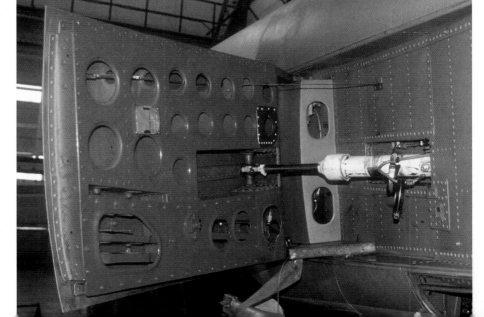

▸ Israeli A-4M speed brakes are shown in the fully extended position. Speed brakes are used on all versions during landing in order to maintain high engine RPM. The J-52 engine 'spool-up' time is slow enough to create hazardous situations when a go-around is required, hence the necessity to maintain a higher power setting on approach. (Ra'anan Weiss)

▲ Chaff (left) and flare dispensers (right) on an Israeli A-4M. Chaff is a defensive measure against radar-guided missiles, while flares are intended to decoy heat-seeking SAMs. (Ra'anan Weiss)

▲ Head-on view of an IDF A-4M. Landing gear is standard for late-model Skyhawks, but the Israeli Skyhawks have replaced the 20 mm cannon mounted in the wing root with 30 mm cannon mounted under the wings. (Ra'anan Weiss)

◄ The aft-facing KB-18A bomb damage assessment camera on the rear of the port main gear fairing on the IDF A-4M. (Ra'anan Weiss)

▲ American Skyhawks all carried a pair of Colt Mk-12 20 mm cannons in their wing roots. All have top-hinged nose cones.

▲ This A-4C has the typical unique-to-the-Skyhawk boarding ladder installed. The intake ducts on Skyhawk models A, B, C, and L are flush with the fuselage. All other models have ducts separated from the fuselage.

◄ The A-4L is an upgraded version of the A-4C. A-4L upgrades from the C model include IP-936 AXQ Video, STENCEL MOD to the Escapac 1 ejection seat, wing spoilers, AN/ARC-51A communications, APX-64(V) IFF, ARN-52(V) TACAN, and ARA-50 ADF. The large rack attached to the bulkhead contains the RT-743/ARC-51A radio communications receiver-transmitter. (Don Hauler)

▲ Marine Lance Corporal Rodney L. Burroughs of the 1st Marine Air Wing inspects an A-4E of VMA-121 during maintenance on the flight line at Chu Lai, RVN, 1969. (USMC by 1/Lt Joe Collins)

▲ Marines at MCAS Cherry Point, North Carolina, prepare to start an A-4C of VMA-224 on 13 April 1961. They are using the Ground Turbine Compressor (GTC) at left to provide power. (USMC by Tomkins)

▸ A-4E of VMA-331 at Milwaukee, July 1966. (R.M. Hill)

19

▲ A fledgling Naval Aviator checks with deck handlers during his initial carrier qualification aboard USS *America* (CV-66) in 1992. Students fly from the front seat on all but instrument training hops. The instrument training hood can be seen retracted at the back of the rear cockpit. During training this is pulled forward to obscure all outside visual cues. The large TA-4 canopy affords excellent visibility for both student and instructor. (Lou Drendel)

▸ Nose boom of this TA-4J at NATC contains test instrumentation. (Lou Drendel)

▾ A TA-4J of VT-7 aboard USS *America*. Ownership of this one is claimed by the Marines!

TA-4Js of the Test Pilot School (TPC) at Naval Air Test Center, Patuxent River, Maryland, are used to teach student test pilots proper test procedures for new aircraft. All contain special instrumentation for this mission.

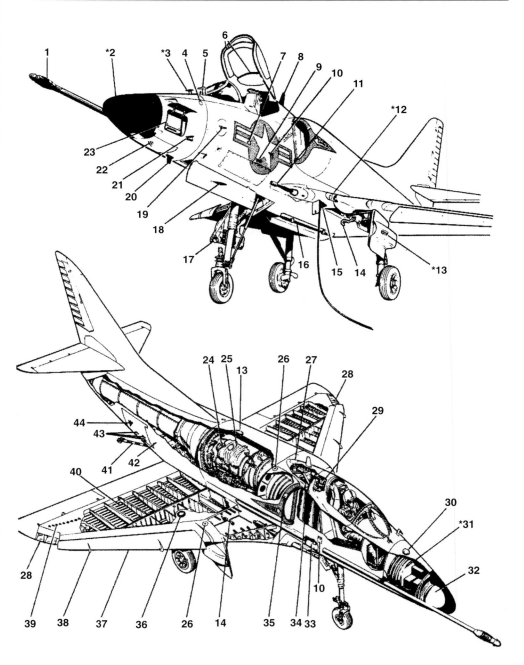

A-4C at NATC in 1969. A, B, C, E, and L models of the Skyhawk do not have nose wheel steering. The white shield at the rear of the canopy was a nuclear blast shield, meant to protect retreating pilots after LABS delivery of nuclear weapons.

A-4C Features

1. Air refueling probe
2. Radome
3. Total temperature sensor
4. Brake fluid level window
5. Pitot tube
6. Thermal radiation closure
7. Oxygen overboard vent
8. UHF radio antenna
9. Normal cockpit entry handle
10. External canopy jettison handle
11. 20 millimeter guns
12. Angle-of-attack approach light
13. Anticollision light
14. Catapult hooks
15. External power receptacle and access doors
16. Four-hook ejector rack assembly
17. Taxi light
18. Missile guidance antenna (when carried)
19. Angle-of-attack vane and transducer
20. TACAN antenna
21. Static orifice
22. UHF-ADF antenna cover
23. Nose compartment access door

24. Oil tank filler cap
25. Oil tank
26. Fuel nozzle grounding receptacle
27. Fuselage fuel tank filler cap
28. Wing position lights
29. Cockpit canopy air bungee cylinder
30. IFF-SIF radar identification antenna
31. AN/ASQ-17 integrated electronics center
32. Radar transmitter and receiver group
33. Emergency generator
34. Fuselage fuel tank
35. Air refueling probe light
36. Wing tank filler cap
37. Slat
38. Barricade engagement detent
39. Vortex generators
40. Integral wing fuel tank
41. Arresting hook
42. JATO igniter terminal
43. JATO mounting hooks
44. Speedbrake

*A-4C only

▲ An A-4C of VMA-225 being 'bombed up' for a practice sortie at MCAS Cherry Point, North Carolina. VMA-225 became the first Marine squadron to deploy and conduct night operations aboard USS *Enterprise* (CVN-65), spending the last three months of 1962 aboard the 'Big E' during the Cuban Missile crisis.

A pair of A-4E Skyhawks of VA-56 accompany an EA-3B Skywarrior of VAH-4. All were aboard the USS *Ticonderoga* (CVA-14) for a 1965/66 Westpac (Vietnam) cruise. (US Navy)

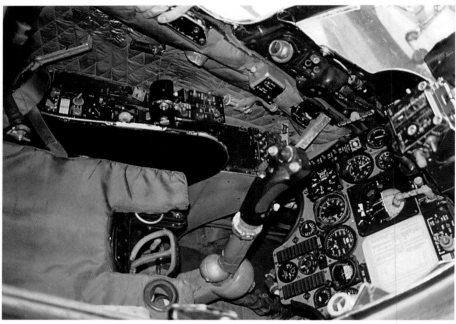

▲ The cockpit of a Top Gun A-4M.

◀ The top of the panel is dominated by the gunsight and Angle of Attack (AOA) Indexer and Approach Power Compensator Light.

▼ A Naval Aviation Student pilot awaits his turn on the catapult aboard USS *America* during carrier qualifications. His hands are on top of the panel to reassure deck handlers there will be no inadvertent switch-throwing.

The cockpit of the TA-4J with standard analog flight instruments. The left console contains throttle, flaps, speed brakes, landing gear, engine control panel, oxygen and anti-G system panel, canopy opening handle and some radar controls. The instrument panel is dedicated to flight and engine instruments, navigation displays with gunsight and AOA indexer above. The right console contains environmental controls, lighting controls, and nav/com panels. (Ted Carlson Fotodynamics)

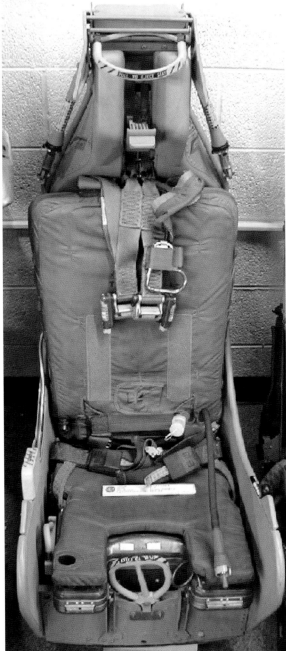

The A-4 uses the Escapac 1C-3 ejection seat. The primary activation handle is the face curtain pull atop the seat. The secondary handle is between the pilots legs. As with most modern U.S. jets, the parachute is integral to the seat and is attached to the pilot's torso harness once he is in the seat.

Cockpit Details

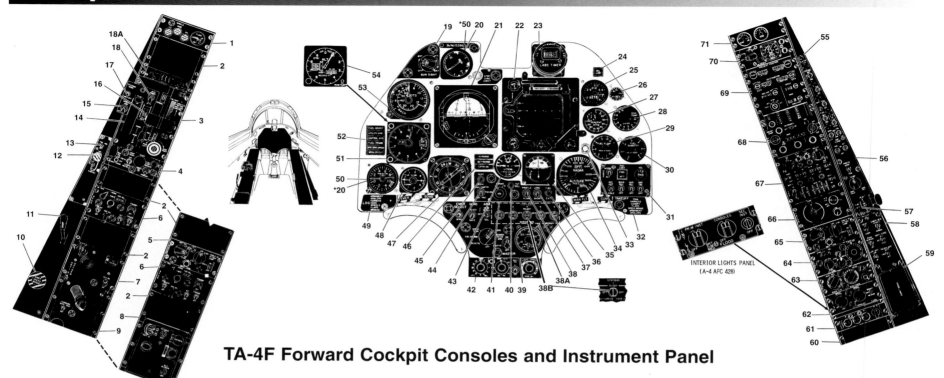

TA-4F Forward Cockpit Consoles and Instrument Panel

A-4 AFC 387

1. Wheels and flaps position indicators
2. Blank panel
3. Throttle panel
4. Engine control panel
5. Radar control panel (A-4 AFC 387)
6. Autopilot control panel
7. Oxygen and anti-G panel
8. Oxygen, anti-G, exposure suit controls
9. Anti-exposure suit control panel
10. Emergency speedbrake control
11. Canopy control panel
12. Manual fuel shutoff control lever
13. Smoke abatement switch
14. Flap handle
15. Spoiler arm switch
16. JATO jettison switch
17. Nosewheel steering switch
18. JATO arm switch
18A. ASW-25A control panel

19. Gunsight panel
20. Angle-of-attack indicator
21. All-attitude indicator
22. Radar scope
23. LABS timer
24. Oil quantity indicator switch
25. Pressure ratio indicator
26. Oil pressure indicator
27. Tachometer
28. Exhaust temperature indicator
29. Fuel flow indicator
30. Fuel quantity indicator
31. ICS and radio control panel
32. Takeoff checklist
33. Radar altimeter low altitude warning light
34. Radar altimeter
35. Standby attitude indicator
36. Fuel int-ext switch
37. Radar long-short switch

38. Radar profile-plan switch
38A. Sta select switches
38B. Sta 3 (centerline) switch
39. Armament panel
40. Target reject switch
41. Shrike volume switch
42. Aircraft weapons release system panel
43. Liquid oxygen quantity indicator
44. BHDI, nav computer TACAN-NAVPAC switch
45. Test switch
46. Pilot's advisory lights
47. Bearing-distance-heading indicator
48. Vertical velocity indicator
49. Landing checklist
50. Accelerometer
51. Altimeter
52. Caution panel
53. Airspeed indicator
54. AAU-19A altimeter

55. Exterior lights panel
56. Air conditioning panel
57. TACAN control switch/indicator
58. Miscellaneous switches panel
59. Spare lamps container
60. Blank panel
61. AFCS test panel
62. interior lights panel
63. Auxiliary UHF control panel
64. Compass control panel
65. Radar control panel
66. TACAN control panel
67. IFF control panel
68. UHF control panel
69. Navigation computer control panel
70. Doppler radar control panel
71. Trim position indicator panel

*A-4 AFC 451

Cockpit Details

ESCAPAC 1C-3 Ejection Seat

1. Harness reset manual detent pin
2. Firing pin shear
3. lap belt pin
4. Seat actuator
5. Nitrogen storage bottle for separation bladder operation
6. Rocket catapult
7. Lower ejection handle
8. Lower separation bladder
9. Emergency restraint release handle
10. Parachute arming lanyard channel
11. Upper separation bladder

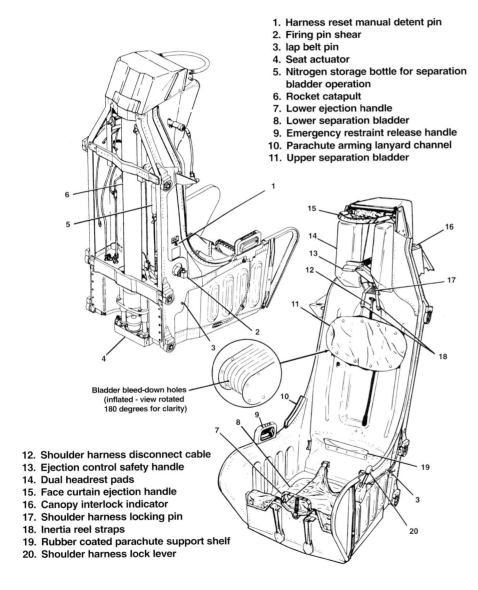

Bladder bleed-down holes (inflated - view rotated 180 degrees for clarity)

12. Shoulder harness disconnect cable
13. Ejection control safety handle
14. Dual headrest pads
15. Face curtain ejection handle
16. Canopy interlock indicator
17. Shoulder harness locking pin
18. Inertia reel straps
19. Rubber coated parachute support shelf
20. Shoulder harness lock lever

A-4L seat showing safety ribbon installation. The latest version of the A-4 ejection seat provided 'zero-zero' capability (successful ejection/survival ensured at zero airspeed and zero altitude). (Don Hauler)

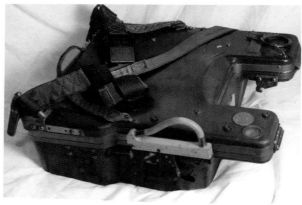

▲ The survival pack contained in the A-4 ejection seat contained elementary survival gear such as water, medical supplies, dye packs, shark repellant, and life raft.

▸ A-4M instrument panel.

▾ A-4M right console.

◂ Detail of the A-4M ejection seat top.

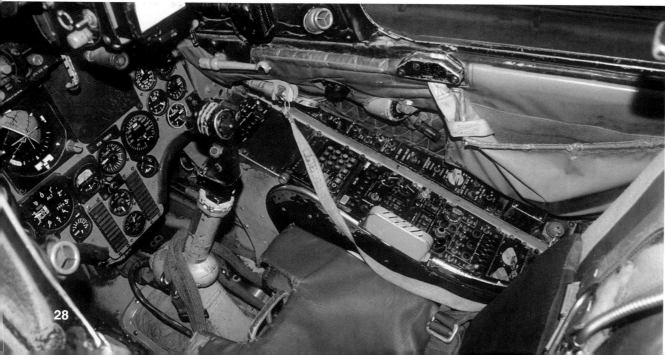

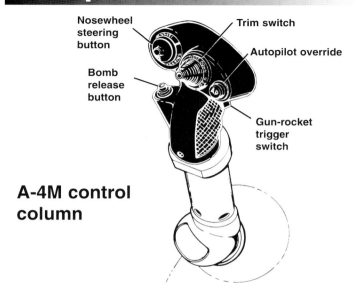

Cockpit Details

Nosewheel steering button

Trim switch

Autopilot override

Bomb release button

Gun-rocket trigger switch

A-4M control column

Israeli A-4M cockpit details. The IDF operates primarily in a visual flight rules (VFR) environment, and their Skyhawks are not generally equipped with sophisticated IFR navigation aids. (Ra'anan Weiss)

▲ TA-4J cockpit canopy profile demonstrates the visibility afforded the instructor pilot from the rear cockpit. (Ted Carlson Fotodynamics)

▲ A-4L cockpit details. One hundred A-4Cs were modified to 'L' standard for use by the Naval
◄ Reserves. First flight of the A-4L was 21 August 1969. Modifications included an uprated J-65 engine, split flaps with spoilers, and updated electronic gear housed in the fuselage 'hump,' a la A-4F standard. The series of lights under the lip of the glare shield include LABS indicator light, OBST warning light, Remote Channel Indicator, and Low Altitude Warning System Lights. (Don Hauler)

IDF A-4M seat (port side) with instruction. (Ra'anan Weiss)

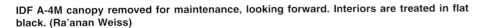

IDF A-4M canopy removed for maintenance, looking forward. Interiors are treated in flat black. (Ra'anan Weiss)

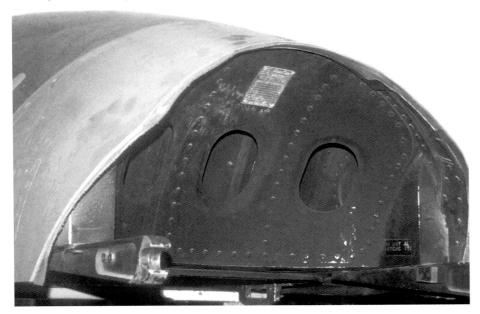

Inside rear view of the IDF A-4M canopy, looking over the top of the Escapac ejection seat. Warning ribbons lettered in Hebrew safety the seat firing mechanisms. (Ra'anan Weiss)

Windscreen of an IDF A-4M. The pitot tube/temperature sensor is adjacent to the windscreen rain dispersion outlet. Pressurized air is directed over the windscreen to keep it clear of rain. (Ra'anan Weiss)

Left-hand console of the IDF A-4M, showing oxygen system hoses (bottom) and the canopy control handle (inside the loop of the hose). Yellow striped handle at top is the emergency fuel shutoff. (Ra'anan Weiss)

Additional details of the left console include the throttle and control panel forward of the throttle, which contains the rain repellent button, Spoiler Arm-Off Switch. The JATO Control Panel of USMC Skyhawks has been replaced by Chaff dispenser button, BDA camera control, and nose wheel steering switch. The panel immediately behind the throttle is dedicated to fuel management, while the panel behind that contains the autopilot controls. (Ra'anan Weiss)

Control stick contains "coolie hat" in the center for trim (aileron and elevator), trigger for guns/rockets, buttons for bomb release and autopilot override. The paddle switch in front of the stick typically controls nose wheel steering. (Ra'anan Weiss)

▲ Canopy of an IDF TA-4J.

▸ IDF A-4M ejection seat. When the face curtain on the ejection seat is pulled, the pilot's harness is automatically retracted, ensuring the proper posture during ejection. Canopy separation occurs immediately, followed by firing of the rocket seat. Within one second, automatic separation from the seat occurs. Emergency oxygen is provided and a barostat inflates the parachute at a preset altitude. (Ra'anan Weiss)

▼ Left cockpit console of an IDF Skyhawk. (Ra'anan Weiss)

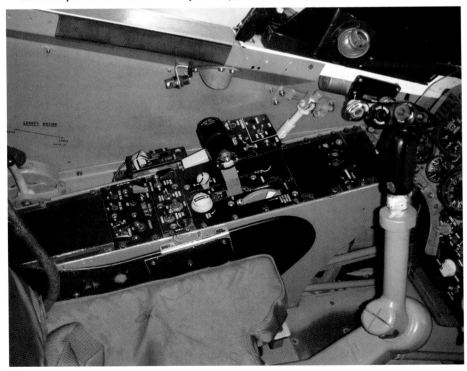

WARNING

JET

INTAKE

RESCUE

The J-52-P-408 engine is rated at 11,200 pounds thrust (what the engine will develop during sea level static operation on a standard atmospheric day, with a bellmouth inlet duct and no aircraft accessories installed). There is an inlet anti-icing system, intercompressor stall air bleed system, self-contained lubrication system, fuel system, ignition system, and fuel heater. The principle intake differences between A-4A, B, and C models and later versions is the 'split' between intake and fuselage. A TA-4J intake is at left, with the A-4A at right. The compressor airbleed system vents low-pressure compressor unit air overboard as necessary to prevent overloading the high pressure compressor unit. The static port (below and to the left of the 'Rescue' arrow) must be kept clear to allow this and prevent compressor stalls. (Lou Drendel)

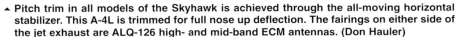

▲ Pitch trim in all models of the Skyhawk is achieved through the all-moving horizontal stabilizer. This A-4L is trimmed for full nose up deflection. The fairings on either side of the jet exhaust are ALQ-126 high- and mid-band ECM antennas. (Don Hauler)

▲ A-4Ms also carried ALQ-126 high- and mid-band ECM. The ALR-45 homing and warning antenna is contained in the pod on top of the vertical fin. (Ted Carlson Fotodynamics)

◄ The tail section of a VMA-311 'Tomcats' A-4E removed for engine change at Chu Lai, Vietnam in December 1967. VMA-311 flew 54,625 combat sorties during the Vietnam War, from 1965 to 1972. (USMC)

▲ JATO bottle installation on an A-4B (A4D-2) of VMA-331. (Jim Hawkins via John Gourley)

▼ The A-4M was the first Skyhawk to be equipped with a brake chute, in deference to the Marines' need for short field landings. (Ted Carlson Fotodynamics)

▲ A 'Top Gun' A-4E on approach to NAS Miramar with speed brakes fully deployed. Late model Skyhawks (including upgraded versions of the E and F) had the pitot static probe installed on the vertical fin. (Ted Carlson Fotodynamics)

▼ The IDF A-4M brake chute housing is slightly different. (right, Ra'anan Weiss)

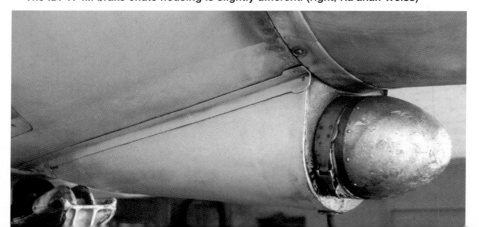

Israeli tails, of the 'Flying Wing' Squadron (left) and the 'Flying Tigers' Squadron (above). After the 1973 Yom Kippur War all Israeli Skyhawks were equipped with a tail pipe extension to provide a measure of protection against heat-seeking missiles. The extension length is 101 cm with an opening width of 54.7 cm. (Ra'anan Weiss)

The standard TA-4J exhaust.

A-4M Antenna Locations

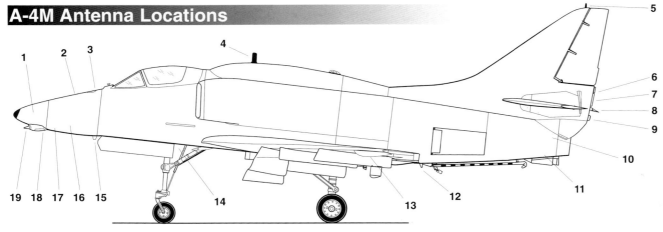

1. AN/APG-53 radar antenna
2. AN/APX-72 IFF forward antenna
3. Missile guidance antenna
4. AN/ARC-51A UHF radio antenna
5. AN/APN-154(V) radar beacon antenna
6. AN/ALQ-100 ECM receive aft antenna
7. AN/ARN-52(V) TACAN aft antenna
8. AN/ALQ-100 ECM transmitter absorber
9. AN/ALQ-100 ECM pulse transmitter aft antenna
10. AN/APR-25(V) ECM receiver aft antenna (2)

11. AN/APX-72 IFF aft antenna
12. AN/ARW-67 antenna
13. Radar altimeter (under left wing outboard)
14. AN/ALQ-100 ECM pulse transmitter forward antenna
15. AN/ARN-52(V) TACAN forward antenna
16. AN/ARA-50 UHF-ADF antenna
17. AN-APN-153(V) Doppler antenna
18. AN/APR-25(V) ECM receiver forward antenna (2)
19. AN/ALQ-100 ECM receiver forward antenna

▲ IDF A-4M aft fuselage detail. (Ra'anan Weiss)

▼ Avionics 'hump' on a Top Gun A-4M (Lou Drendel)

▼ Skyhawk intake plug detail. Intake plugs are red with white stencils. Handle is natural aluminum. (Lou Drendel)

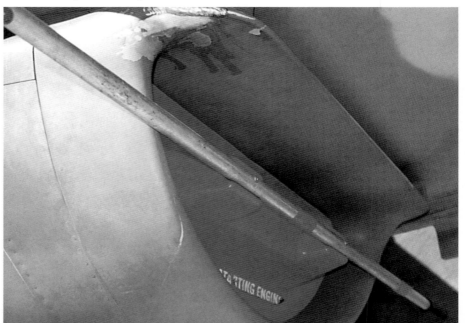

Zero-Zero Ejection Seat

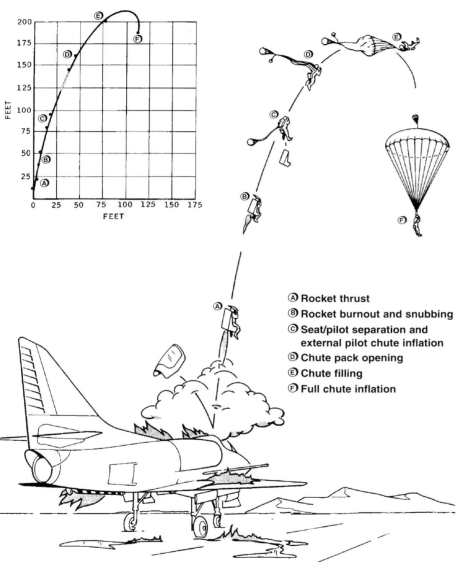

(A) Rocket thrust
(B) Rocket burnout and snubbing
(C) Seat/pilot separation and external pilot chute inflation
(D) Chute pack opening
(E) Chute filling
(F) Full chute inflation

▲ A-4L port fuselage. (Don Hauler)

▼ TA-4J aft fuselage with reinforcement applied below and forward of the BuNo. (Lou Drendel)

A-4F of VA-153 'Blue Tail Flies' in 1968, while assigned to CVW-15 aboard USS *Coral Sea* (CVA-43). This was the last model of the Skyhawk flown by VA-153, which transitioned to the A-7A in 1969. It is loaded with 300-gallon external fuel tanks on stations 2 and 4.

A pristine, factory-fresh A-4F for the Marines in standard Gloss Gull Gray top and Gloss White undersurfaces.

A-4G N-13 154907 of the Royal Australian Navy. The RAN operated two squadrons of Skyhawks: VF-805, an operational squadron deployed aboard the aircraft carrier HMAS *Melbourne*, and VC-724, a training squadron. The Australian A-4G was generally similar to the A-4E but powered by a 9,300 lb thrust J52-P-8A. Eight A-4Gs were delivered in 1967. Australian Skyhawks retained their US Navy BuNos but with the prefix 'N-13.'

In 1961 the RAN received eight ex-US Navy A-4Fs including this one (BuNo 155061). After HMAS *Melbourne* was withdrawn from service in 1984, the surviving Australian A-4s were sold to New Zealand.

The Royal New Zealand Air Force received ten A-4K and 4 TA-4K Skyhawks in 1970. The Kiwi Skyhawks essentially were A-4F airframes, including the 'hump back' avionics package and modified to include drag chutes, APX-72 IFF antennae, and Sidewinder air-to-air missile capability. An additional 10 Skyhawks (eight A-4Gs and two TA-4Gs) were purchased from Australia in 1984. From 1985 to 1989, New Zealand conducted a major Skyhawk upgrade program, installing 'glass' cockpits, HUDs (Head Up Displays), and new radars and navigation systems, removing the avionics 'hump,' re-sparring wings, and upgrading landing gear and control surfaces. New Zealand's A-4s were retired in 2001. NZ6216 was a former Australian A-4G (BuNo 155061).

Tie-down Locations

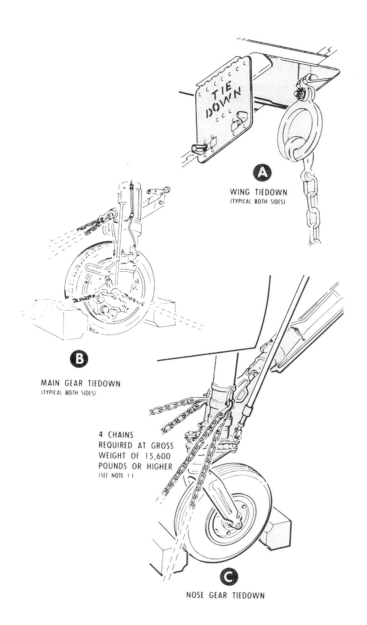

A WING TIEDOWN
(TYPICAL BOTH SIDES)

B MAIN GEAR TIEDOWN
(TYPICAL BOTH SIDES)

4 CHAINS
REQUIRED AT GROSS
WEIGHT OF 15,600
POUNDS OR HIGHER
(SEE NOTE 1)

C NOSE GEAR TIEDOWN

▲ A-4E of VMA-223 performing a JATO takeoff from Chu Lai in 1966. Short runways required use of JATO or catapults as well as field arresting gear. (USMC)

▼ A-4C of VA-34 'Blue Blasters' at Danang, Republic of Vietnam, in 1967. Ground power unit is USAF issue and atypical for use with the Skyhawk. VA-34 made one combat cruise during the Vietnam War, on USS *Intrepid* (CVS-11).

An A-4C of VMA-131 on approach with 300-gallon wing tanks. Main gear retracts forward, rotating to lie flat in the wheel wells. Nose gear retracts forward. Anti-collision lights are on rear of main gear sponsons. (Jim Hawkins via John Gourley)

Marine loading 20 mm cannon on an A-4E at Chu Lai, RVN in 1967. Each Colt Mk 12 cannon carries 100 rounds of ammunition. (USMC)

Fuel capacity of both wing and fuselage internal and three external tanks: 1,800 U.S. gallons. All three fuel tanks seen here are 300 gallon capacity. The centerline is a 'Buddy' refueling pod, capable of transferring fuel at the rate of 200 gallons per minute.

TA-4J nose gear. Nose wheel steering mechanism is next to the oleo shock tube. (Ted Carlson Fotodynamics)

TA-4J main gear. Red ribbons are attached to safety pins, which prevent inadvertent retraction of the gear on the ground. (Ted Carlson Fotodynamics)

▲ A Skyhawk on final approach with 'everything hanging out.'

▼ Nose wheel well of an IDF A-4M. (Ra'anan

▲ Starboard forward main gear door with landing light.

◀ IDF A-4M nose gear showing detail of nose wheel steering mechanism.

▼ Aft main gear door. IDF Skyhawks have all landing gear and gear door interiors painted gloss white with red edging. (Ra'anan Weiss)

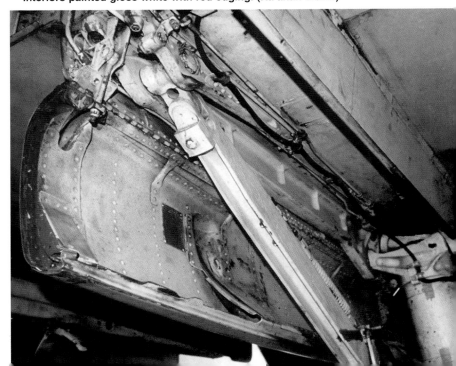

Skyhawk Evolution

XA4D-1

A-4A

A-4B

A-4C (A-4L)

A-4L avionics 'hump'

A-4F

A-4F

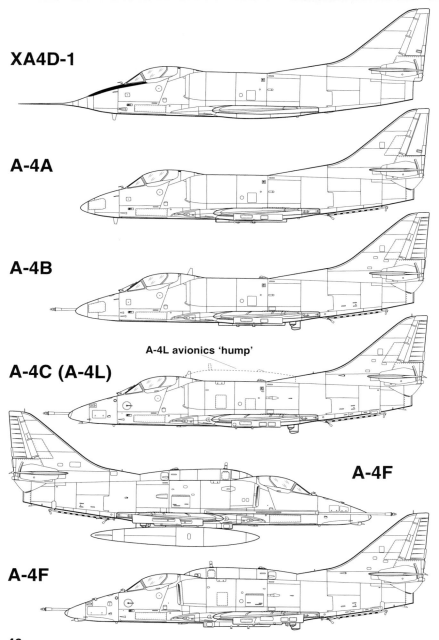

TA-4F

A-4H (A-4K)

A-4M

A-4N

A-4S

TA-4S

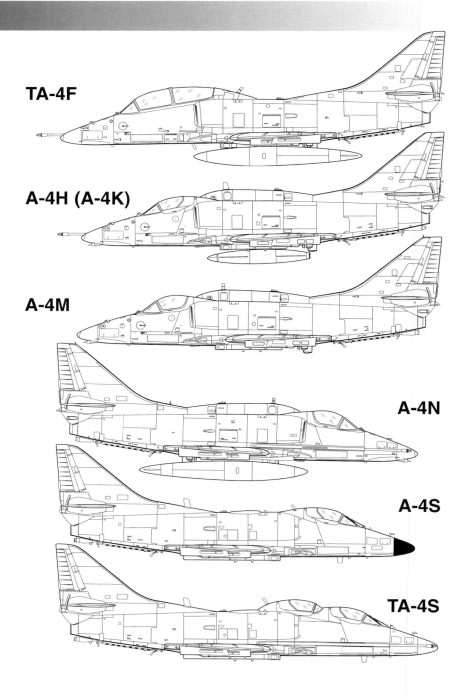

A-4E

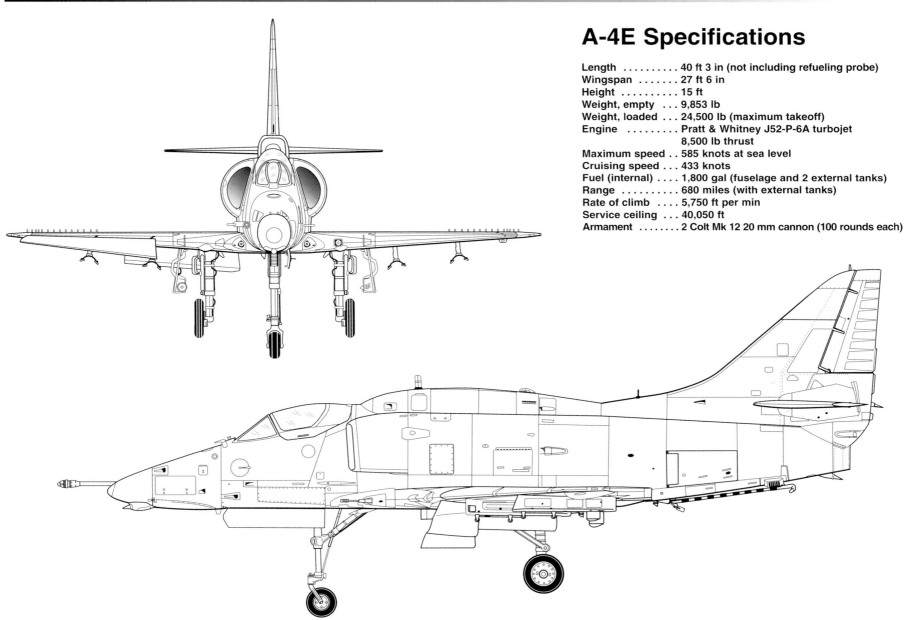

A-4E Specifications

Length .... 40 ft 3 in (not including refueling probe)
Wingspan .... 27 ft 6 in
Height .... 15 ft
Weight, empty ... 9,853 lb
Weight, loaded ... 24,500 lb (maximum takeoff)
Engine .... Pratt & Whitney J52-P-6A turbojet
　　　　　　　　　　 8,500 lb thrust
Maximum speed .. 585 knots at sea level
Cruising speed ... 433 knots
Fuel (internal) .... 1,800 gal (fuselage and 2 external tanks)
Range .... 680 miles (with external tanks)
Rate of climb .... 5,750 ft per min
Service ceiling ... 40,050 ft
Armament .... 2 Colt Mk 12 20 mm cannon (100 rounds each)

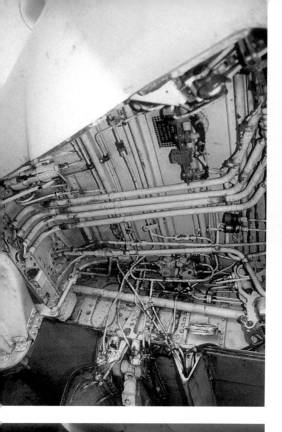

◄ Main gear wheel well of an Israeli A-4M. (Ra'anan Weiss)

▲ Main gear wheel well of a TA-4J.

▶ The yellow hook is the catapult bridle attachment point for carrier operations.

◄ Forward port main gear door exterior, TA-4J.

▼ Interior of the forward port main gear door on a TA-4J.

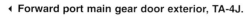

▼ Tailhook attach point of a TA-4J.

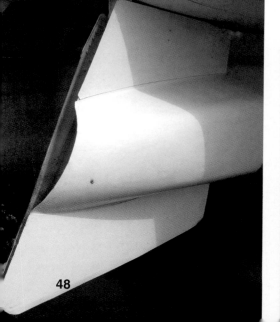

▲ This A-4E at NATC Patuxent River in 1969 has its flaps down and fuselage belly access panel open. (Lou Drendel)

▸ A-4C about to trap. Long oleo extensions cushion rough landings. The landing gear is retracted and extended by utility hydraulic system pressure. The gear telescopes to allow it to fit in the wheel wells. When retracted, the landing gear is held up by utility hydraulic pressure and, in the case of hydraulic system failure, the gear rests on the landing gear doors which are held closed by mechanical latches. For emergency extension, the latches are manually released by the pilot. (Harry Gann)

▾ This A-4C of VA-36 'Roadrunners' wore the patch of the Tonkin Gulf Yacht Club on the vertical fin during the Vietnam combat cruise of CVW-10 aboard USS *Intrepid* from 4 June 1968 to 8 February 1969. A-4C units bore the brunt of much of the early air campaign against North Vietnam.

▾ The 'Tonkin Gulf Yacht Club' was a whimsical reference to squadrons operating on Yankee Station in the Gulf of Tonkin during the Vietnam War. This was their patch.

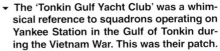

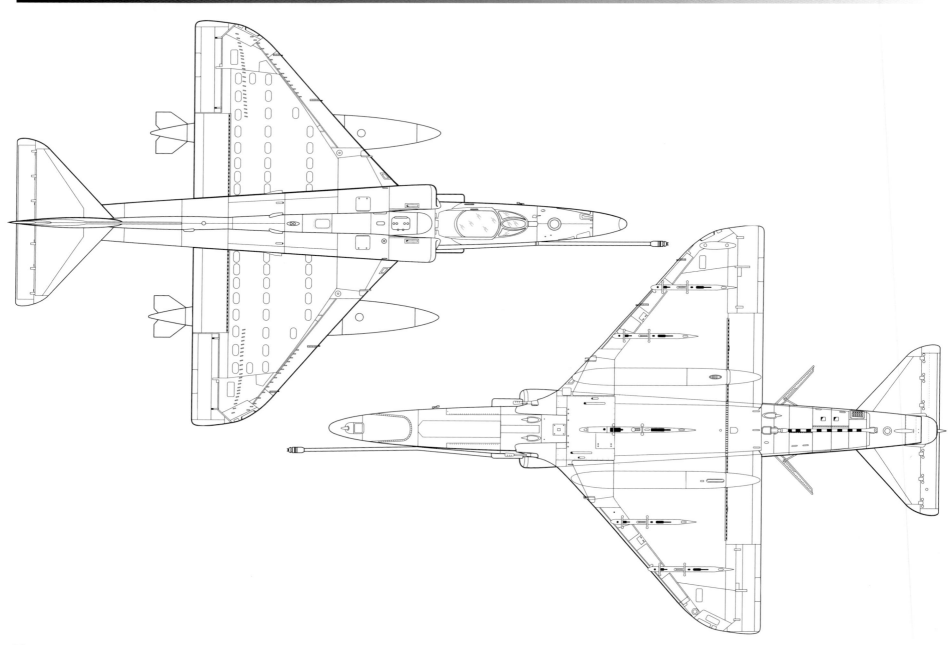

A-4E

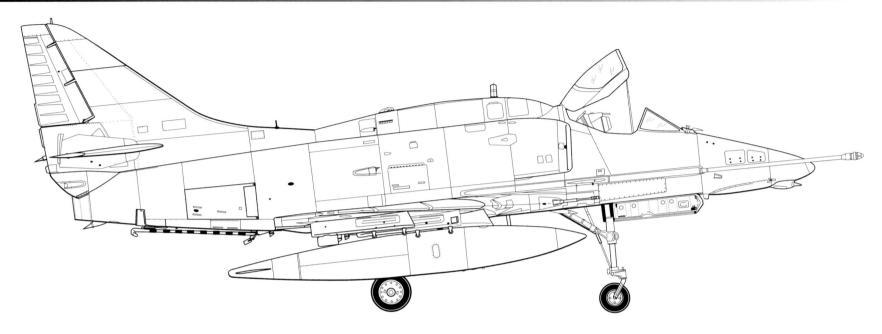

OA-4M

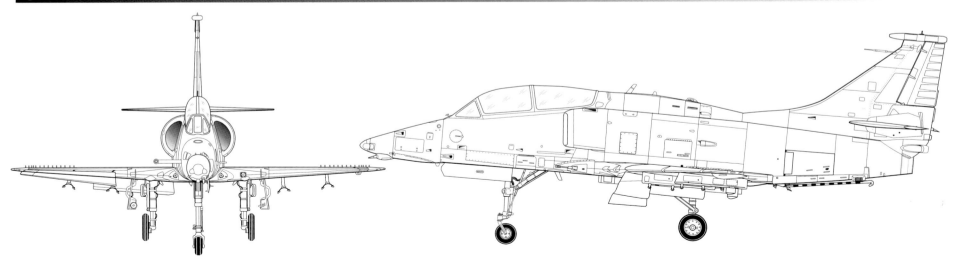

An A-4M of VMA-324 during an early test of the AGM-62 Walleye TV-guided bomb. VMA-324 was the first unit to operate the A-4M, receiving their first aircraft on 26 February 1971. Six US Marine Corps squadrons flew the Skyhawk before it was replaced by AV-8 Harriers and F/A-18 Hornets. The A-4M was specifically developed for the Marine Corps, which could not afford to buy the A-7 Corsair II, which replaced the Skyhawk in Navy service. The first big upgrade from the A-4F was the J-52-P-408A engine, with 11,200 lb thrust, a 20 percent increase over the A-4F engine. This translated to improved performance as well as an increased weapons load. Original A-4Ms were equipped with APG-53 radar, which necessitated modification of the refueling probe, 'cranking' it outboard so that it didn't interfere with the radar. The A-4M nose was further modified by the addition of the Hughes Angle/Rate Bombing System (ARBS), which enabled use of laser-guided 'smart' bombs. A-4Ms served with active-duty Marine squadrons until 1990, and with the reserves until 1994. (Harry Gann)

‹ Detail of the nose gear on an Israeli A-4M. (Ra'anan Weiss)

› Israeli A-4M main landing gear inboard view. (Ra'anan Weiss)

▲ A pair of A-4Ms from VMA-331 'Bumblebees' drops practice bombs on the range. Distinguishing characteristics of the A-4M are the larger canopy profile, squared off vertical fin with APN-154(V) Radar Beacon Antenna, and drag chute housing under the tailpipe. (Harry Gann)

▸ A nearly 'stock' A-4M, BuNo 159486, on the flight-line at NAS Miramar while serving with the U.S. Navy Fighter Weapons School ('Top Gun'). The centerline station was used to carry an Air Combat Maneuvering Instrumentation (ACMI) pod which transmitted real-time dogfight data to the Top Gun control center. Aggressor squadrons throughout the Navy and Air Force used a variety of camouflage schemes to reflect potential real-world adversaries. (Ted Carlson Fotodynamics)

A disassembled A-4M wing sans leading edge slats, flaps, ailerons, and a portion of the tip section. As evidenced by the absence of skin over the flap area, this wing is from a spoiler-equipped Skyhawk. Spoilers were introduced on the A-4F. The wing slats open automatically under various flight conditions to improve airflow characteristics over the wing. As the two slats operate independently, and aerodynamically, one may occasionally open slightly in advance of the other, imposing a rolling movement. Because they are spring-loaded, they are always open on the ground.

▲ The starboard leading edge wingtip on a TA-4J.

◄ The A-4M wing is festooned with vortex generators, which improve airflow over the ailerons, making them more effective at high angles of attack. Trim tabs on the trailing edges of the ailerons help to keep the stick centered under asymmetric load conditions.

▲ Top view of the extended leading edge slat. A pair of boundary layer fences on the leading edges of the slats directs the airflow over the wing. (Lou Drendel)

▼ Port wing tip on an A-4M. The large bulge under the wingtip contains the radar altimeter. (Lou Drendel)

▲ Underside view of the extended leading edge slats and their actuators. Relative positions of the leading edges of the two wing pylons is evident. (Ted Carlson Fotodynamics)

◄ Front view of the extended leading edge slat. The square area in the center of the black wingwalk leading edge contains the approach lights.(Lou Drendel)

▲ Fully extended flaps of an Israeli A-4M. This is the setting used for landing; half flaps are recommended for all takeoffs, but flaps-up takeoffs are permitted as long as the tire limit of 175 knots is not exceeded (Ra'anan Weiss)

▲ TA-4J leading edge slats in full-out position.

◄ Rear view of vortex generators on TA-4J wing.

▼ Multiple Ejector Rack (MER) loaded with 25 pound practice bombs. (Ted Carlson Fotodynamics)

▼ TA-4J tailhook. Retraction and extension of the hook are accomplished by a pneumatic-hydraulic holddown cylinder in the aft engine compartment. (Lou Drendel)

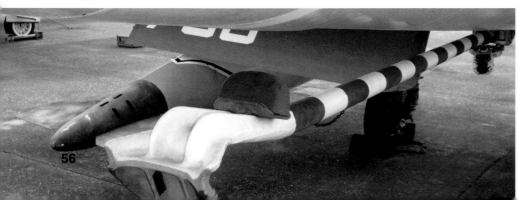

A-4E of VMA-121 at Chu Lai, Republic of Vietnam, loaded with Mk-117 750-pound bombs and Mk 80 series Snakeye bombs. VMA-121 flew the Skyhawk in Vietnam from 1966 to 1969, when they converted to the A-6 Intruder. (USMC)

A-4F of VA-55, loaded with LAU-32A/A 2.75-inch folding fin aerial rocket (FFAR) pod on outboard station, Mk-81 Snakeye bombs inboard.

A-4E of VA-163 heading into North Vietnam with a load of Snakeye bombs. VA-163 flew from USS *Oriskany* on this combat cruise.

▲ Marine of VMA-311 loading a Mk-82 Snakeye on an A-4E at Chu Lai, Republic of Vietnam, 1967. VMA-311 was one of the first Marine squadrons to arrive in country in May 1965. (USMC)

▲ Marine loads 20 mm rounds in an A-4E of VMA-331 at Chu Lai, December 1967. Each gun weighed 88 pounds. (USMC)

◄ Marine armorer of MAG-12 disconnects expended LAU-10/A Rocket Launcher tubes at Chu Lai in December 1967. The LAU-10/A launcher was loaded with four 5-inch Zuni FFARs. Pods were 139.5 inches long and weighed 533 pounds loaded. (USMC)

▲ An A4D-2N (A-4C) loaded with AGM-12C Bullpup missiles during testing at NATC Patuxent River, Maryland. The Bullpup weighed 1,785 pounds and used a 30,000-pound thrust liquid-fuel rocket engine to achieve a range of ten miles. The pilot guided the missile by watching the position of tail-mounted tracking flares in relation to his line-of-sight view of the target.

▶ Loading Napalm at MAG-12, Chu Lai, Republic of Vietnam, December 1967. Napalm is jellied gasoline and must be expended once loaded. (USMC)

▼ A-4Es of VMA-121 enroute to targets with AGM-12A/B Bullpups mounted on Aero 5A-1 launchers, which in turn are mounted to Aero 20A-1 Ejector Racks. The Bullpup was manufactured in large numbers, and was used in Vietnam by the USAF and USMC as well as the Navy. It required the pilot to track the missile all the way to the target, limiting his ability to take evasive action. (USMC)

A pair of A-4Fs from VA-94 while assigned to USS *Bon Homme Richard* (CVA-31) during their 1969 combat cruise. 'Bobbie' is the 'CAG bird'.

An A-4E of VMA-121 taxies for takeoff at Chu Lai, loaded with Mk-81 Snakeyes and a 300-gallon centerline tank. (USMC)

An A-4F of VA-192 while assigned to CVW 19, USS *Ticonderoga* (CVA-14) during 1968-69. This is the squadron commander's aircraft.

▲ All IDF Skyhawks were fitted with the tailpipe extension after the 1973 Yom Kippur War, in which SAM-7 shoulder-launched heat-seeking missiles became a serious threat. The 'Flying Wing' Squadron is one of the oldest in the IDF, dating to the 1956 Suez War, when it was equipped with P-51 Mustangs. (Ra'anan Weiss)

▼ An A-4N of the Israeli Air Force 'Flying Wing' Squadron. It is fitted with the Hughes AN/ABS-19 Angle Rate Bombing System (ARBS) which allows it to deliver the Paveway Mk 80 series laser guided bombs loaded on the wing pylons.

▼ The Israeli Skyhawk is armed with two 30 mm DEFA 553 cannon, each with 150 rounds. The larger 30 mm cannon requires an additional underwing fairing. (Ra'anan Weiss)

▲ Zuni rocket pods staged and ready for loading on Skyhawks aboard USS *Franklin D. Roosevelt* (CVA-42) on 31 October 1966. (US Navy)

▲ An A4D-2 (A-4C) of VMA-211, seen here at El Toro MCAS in 1960 with a variety of bomb loads. VMA-211 transitioned to the Skyhawk in September 1957. (USMC)

◀ A-4E of VMA-311 with a mixed load of Snakeyes and Napalm during a 1969 close support mission over South Vietnam. VMA-311 flew the Skyhawk in combat from 1965 to 1972, logging 54,625 combat sorties. (USMC)

An A-4E of VMA-331 'Tomcats' taxies for takeoff at Chu Lai. It is loaded with Mk-82 'slick' (non-retarded) free-fall bombs. Most Marine missions were flown in the northern South Vietnam area, and several Skyhawks were shot down. (USMC

A deck handler aboard USS *Franklin D. Roosevelt* (CVA-42) directs the pilot of an A-4E of VA-12 onto the port forward catapult. Lack of nosewheel steering requires the use of a tow bar to make finite corrections enroute to catapult hookup. VA-12 participated in several Alpha Strikes against North Vietnam in August and September 1966. (U.S. Navy)

Barrel of the 20 mm Colt Mk-12 cannon mounted in the wing root fairing of all US Skyhawks. The two cannons had 100 rounds each, which could be fired at the rate of 1,000 rounds per minute.

VMA-331 A-4E in a revetment at Danang AB, RVN, in June 1972. It is loaded with Mk-80 series low drag bombs. VMA-331 had returned to South Vietnam to provide support for the ARVN countering the North Vietnamese Easter Offensive. (USMC)

▲ TA-4J of VF-126, the Pacific Fleet adversary training squadron. A total of 241 TA-4s were manufactured. Well-known Soviet camouflage schemes were used on adversary aircraft.

▼ TA-4J of VX-4 at Nellis AFB, April 1976. VX-4 was commissioned at NAS Point Mugu on 11 September 1952. It was dedicated to the operational test and evaluation of fighter aircraft and systems destined for fleet units. It was disestablished in 1992. (Lou Drendel)

▼ The last US Navy unit to fly the Skyhawk was VC-8, based at NAS Roosevelt Roads, Puerto Rico. VC-8 became the AIRLANT fleet adversary squadron in 1997. VC-8 Skyhawks had no radar or radar homing and warning (RHW) equipment, so their primary adversarial duties concentrated on 'at the merge' close-in dogfighting. VC-8 also trained FACs at Roosevelt Roads, using the adjoining Vieques Range. The 'Redtails' were the last U.S. Navy squadron to operate the A-4. The final flight of a Redtails Skyhawk occurred 3 May 2003, and later that year VC-8 was disestablished at NAS Oceana on 23 August.

An A-4C of VA-36. Early model Skyhawks had windshield wipers, while later models used high pressure air to clear the windscreen. Fuselage fuel cell capacity was 1,600 pounds. The antenna on the nose gear door provides missile guidance signals.

VA-216 A-4C after returning from a combat cruise as part of CVW-15 aboard USS Coral Sea from 7 September 1968 to 18 April 1969.

▲ Heavily-laden A-4E of VMA 211 takes off from Chu Lai for a mission in support of the Marine Garrison at Khe Sahn.

▸ Deck handlers position an A-4E of VA-106 on the catapult aboard USS *Intrepid* prior to a combat mission. Lack of nosewheel steering necessitates use of a tow bar. (U.S. Navy)

▾ Chu Lai is 50 miles south of Danang. Starting in April 1965 Navy Seabees worked in 100-degree-plus temperatures to prepare the remote Chu Lai site for an aluminum plank SATS (short airfield for tactical support) 'tinfoil strip' 4,000-foot runway. A catapult and arresting gear were planned to allow Skyhawks to use the field. The arresting gear was installed, but a catapult was not immediately available. JATO (Jet Assisted Take Off) was planned to reduce the Skyhawk takeoff distance by half. A catapult was installed May 14, 1966. This is one of the first tests of the catapult, by an A-4E of VMA-311. (USMC)

A-4E of VA-144 'Road Runners' loaded with Zuni Rocket launchers for a combat mission. From March 18, 1969 to October 29, 1969, the Road Runners flying the Douglas A-4E Skyhawk with CVW-5, embarked on USS *Bon Homme Richard* (CVA 31) for their fifth combat cruise to Vietnam. (US Navy)

▸ A Marine A-4E is prepared for a combat mission from Bien Hoa AB, RVN during the 1972 NVA Easter Offensive. (USMC)

▾ Thirsty Skyhawks line up for refueling behind a KA-3 tanker.

VA-153 emblem

US Marine Corps emblem

A-4B, BuNo 142100, VA-93, Det Q 'Fighting Ravens,' USS *Bennington* (CVS-20), 1964. VA-93's Detachment Q provided daylight fighter protection for the anti-submarine warfare aircraft of CVSG-59.

A-4C, BuNo 147825, VA-153 'Blue Tail Flies,' USS *Coral Sea* (CVA-43), 1965. On its first combat tour to Vietnam as part of CVW-15, Skyhawks of VA-153 participated in Operation ROLLING THUNDER in addition to bombing targets in Laos.

A-4E, BuNo 150095, VMA-331 "Bumblebees,' CVW-8, USS *Forrestal* (CVA-59), Mediter-ranean, 1965.

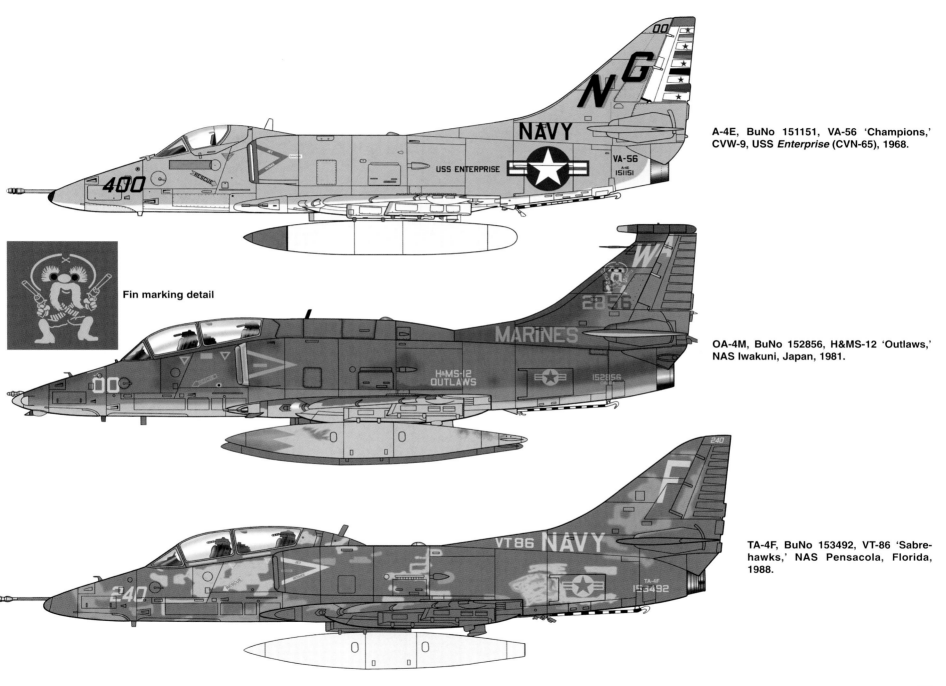

A-4E, BuNo 151151, VA-56 'Champions,'
CVW-9, USS *Enterprise* (CVN-65), 1968.

Fin marking detail

OA-4M, BuNo 152856, H&MS-12 'Outlaws,'
NAS Iwakuni, Japan, 1981.

TA-4F, BuNo 153492, VT-86 'Sabre-
hawks,' NAS Pensacola, Florida,
1988.